Masters of Music

ILLUSTRATED BY RICHARD SHIRLEY SMITH

HAYDN

In the same series
HANDEL
MOZART
BEETHOVEN
TCHAIKOVSKY
DEBUSSY
STRAVINSKY
BRITTEN

Masters of Music

HAYDN

Percy M. Young

Ernest Benn Limited · London
David White · New York

FIRST PUBLISHED 1969
BY ERNEST BENN LIMITED
BOUVERIE HOUSE, FLEET STREET, LONDON EC4
&
DAVID WHITE INC.
60 EAST 55TH STREET, NEW YORK, NY 10022

PRINTED IN GREAT BRITAIN

510-13725-3

LIBRARY OF CONGRESS CATALOG CARD NUMBER
77-96897

Contents

Illustrations

Preface

AMONG THE GREATEST of the world's composers Josef
Haydn is, perhaps, one of the least well known. In this
book many of his works are named, but, even now,
relatively few are at all familiar. Of those that are, however,
the most are among the best loved of musical works. When
one hears symphonies such as the "Surprise" or the
"Clock", or quartets such as the "Emperor", or certain
songs, or the great oratorio *The Creation*, one feels that one
is in the presence of a lively and sympathetic personality
of great warmth.

The music of Haydn, in fact, gives the impression of one
who not only cared about art, but also about people. This is
precisely the kind of man he was. And this is why the story
of his life is so attractive. He was a simple man, of peasant
origin, who never lost sight of the importance of simple
things.

An artist owes much to the place of his birth. Haydn was
always aware of this. To get to know the enchanting part
of Europe of which he was a native is to gain further
insight into the nature of his music. This is why there is a
lot in this book about those places which, while familiar to
him, are little known by people of other lands. Haydn's
friends came from many walks of life. He was respected by
members of all social classes, and admired in many lands. In
late life he was able to visit England where he was especially
honoured and loved. His fame not only spread throughout
Europe but also across the Atlantic, and the popularity of

his symphonies and *The Creation* was a strong and vital influence on the development of musical life in the United States.

Haydn may be seen as the first truly universal composer of modern times. After his death, however, the more obviously romantic, and tragic, biography of his friend Wolfgang Mozart captured the general imagination; and the record of Haydn's life, thought to be somewhat humdrum, was considered of less interest.

But how Haydn lived and how he made the most of the opportunities offered to him, and how he opened up new horizons, is a most exciting story. For it is the story of a man whose genius grew out of perseverance, hard work, and punctuality. In a sense Haydn can inspire all of us, for he was—as is said—a slow starter. The bright boy of the Haydn family was Josef's brother Michael. There is a good deal about him also in this book, because by any standards he was a fine composer, of whose music there is much that is so well worth hearing. Being the brother of his brother he got a very raw deal from history. In trying to put this right to some extent I am, I feel, doing what Josef would have wished. Which tells you some more about one of the world's greatest and most lovable masters of music.

P.M.Y.

1. Country Life

THE LITTLE ONE-STOREY HOUSE in which Josef Haydn was born is now beautifully neat and well-ordered, as befits a museum and a place of pilgrimage for visitors from all over the world. In 1732—Haydn was born on the last day of March in that year—it was indistinguishable from most other peasant cottages in the neighbourhood of the village of Rohrau: squat, too small for any family of those days, isolated by mud during the rainy days of winter, and invaded during summer by the hot dust from the lane outside. Rohrau, now in Austria, lies in the Burgenland—the land of castles—which was once a kind of no-man's land between east and west. Today it is but half-an-hour's drive in one direction into Czechoslovakia. In another direction no more time is needed to reach the Hungarian frontier. In the eighteenth century all these lands were administratively one; part of the Empire of which Vienna was the capital.

In the Burgenland some people spoke Hungarian, others spoke Croat. Most spoke German—though with a strong regional accent—for this was the official language. Educated people—this meant the more intelligent among the aristocracy—also spoke French, which was the language of culture. To the person who only speaks one language there is something essentially romantic about those who can use several. To the traveller in the Burgenland there is, even today, a great fascination in the different languages and dialects that may still be heard there. It is, indeed, altogether a romantic country.

There are hills—the last outliers of the Alps—and rivers. There are great castles on the hills and overlooking the rivers, and castles in the little towns (some of which still have their medieval walls), and castles in the villages. Tucked away between the east and west of Europe the Burgenland escapes the climatic rigours of both. Mostly the weather is warm, even Mediterranean, and the land is fertile. Although far from any coast there is an inland sea, the vast Neusiedler Lake, rich with fish. Still as in Josef Haydn's time brown-faced gipsies, with their own ancient culture, and traditions, and language, live beside this lake. Across the landscape there are many churches, a large number of which are in the rich Baroque style.

In the eighteenth century the lives of the people of this region were controlled by the seasons of the year, by an agricultural economy. Many superstitions, and beliefs, were enshrined in folk-lore and folk-song, the effects of which were inescapable. Together with these beliefs were those which belonged to the Catholic Church. Everywhere there were priests, and members of religious orders, to teach the Faith and also to give help and comfort to those in trouble. Families were large, and closely-knit—clans rather than families, as we understand the term—and once or twice a year each family held its own festival. The citizen of this country owed loyalty to his family, to his Church, to the local overlord, and through him to the Emperor, or Empress. But Vienna was far away. The duke or the count, with his officials, was near at hand. He controlled employment, and determined wages. He dispensed justice— or what passed for justice. He demanded obedience. There were few in the year 1732 who questioned the powers of a

Peasants at work in the Burgenland

count, or a duke, even though during the next half-century there was to be an increasing number of critics of the still largely feudal social order.

The ruler of the village of Rohrau was Count von Harrach, who lived in a not very large, but very charming, castle a mile or so from where the Haydn house is. The Haydns had been long established in the Burgenland. The name means "from the heath"; there is much heathland in the neighbourhood of Rohrau. Matthias Haydn learned the cult of waggon-making and as a young man followed a general practice of those days by travelling from place to place looking for work. He went west as far as Frankfurt on the River Main, and returned to Rohrau in 1727 after ten long years. A conscientious workman, a keen music-lover—he played the harp to the great satisfaction of his neighbours—he set up a waggon-building-and-repairing business with the goodwill of the Count. He fell in love with Anna Maria Koller, one of the cooks in the Castle, and they were married in 1728.

Of this marriage there were twelve children. Seven died in infancy. Of those who survived three became musicians: Franz Josef—the second child; Johann Michael (1737–1806); and Johann Evangelist (1743–1805). The first became one of the greatest composers of all time. The second occupied an honourable place in Austrian music, which would be more evident to us had he not been the brother of a greater genius. Johann Evangelist was less talented and frequently in need of help. Whenever he needed help he knew it would be forthcoming from one or other of his brothers.

Now between the village boy of Rohrau, where there were almost no opportunities for formal education at all, and an acknowledged master of European (and American) music sixty years later there is a great gap. How was this gap filled? Josef Haydn had what is called genius (while his brother Michael had more than average talent). He had determination, and also a rare sense of humour that helped him towards tolerance for and understanding of other people. He was industrious. And so far as his employers were concerned he was prepared to give loyal service. All those factors go some way towards explaining Haydn's success in his career. None of them supply the reason for his undisputed position among the greatest of musicians of all time, and also among the greatest of men. The key word is vision.

The word inspiration is often used in respect of a creative artist. It is a good word provided that its meaning is clear. Haydn described his kind of inspiration for us. In a letter that he wrote to two amateur musicians of Rügen he said that although he often found it difficult to achieve what he set out to achieve an inner voice said to him:

> There are so few happy, contented beings here below—
> they are everywhere dogged by grief and anxiety—
> perhaps your work may now and then become a spring
> from which the man who is careworn or overburdened
> with occupations can draw rest and refreshment for a
> few moments . . .

When he wrote those words Haydn was seventy years old, with undiminished enthusiasm and faith.

Haydn's parents were good people. His father was respected by his neighbours to the extent that he was made the community chairman. The family was brought up to accept the established order of Church and State, and to love music. This, of course, was part of the way of life, and in those days a distinctly musical boy such as Josef—as well as two of his brothers—was not thought to be a problem. On the contrary, he was considered to be well on the way towards a position of decent social standing. But proper teaching was necessary.

Fortunately the half-sister of Matthias Haydn had married a schoolmaster, Matthias Franck, who was the director of a school by the time it was thought desirable for Josef to begin serious instruction. Franck's school was in Hainburg, a little city above the Danube shadowed by the lower Carpathian Mountains and the Hundesheim Hills, dominated by its great castle, and protected by its stout medieval walls and watch-towers, of which three remain to this day. Josef lived in the schoolmaster's house on the "Hungarian" Street, and he learned reading, writing, arithmetic, and how to sing; and to play the harpsichord, the organ, the violin, the trumpet, and the drums. Franck, by reason of his office, was responsible for the music of the church. The young Haydn, conscripted not unwillingly into the choir, learned the basic repertoire of church music—and also how and when to ring the church bells. He lived in a city and neighbourhood that, in summer at least, was gracious and beautiful. He remembered how gaily summer was introduced each May 4 with the Festival in honour of St Florian.

Josef had been a year in Hainburg when the Music Director of the great Cathedral of St Stephen, in Vienna, came that way on a talent-spotting tour. Johann Adam Reutter (1708–72) was a good judge of a voice—which was why he was in charge of the finest choir in the Empire—and when he heard that of Josef Haydn he immediately wanted him as a chorister. Franck supported the idea, and Matthias and Anna Maria Haydn, in Rohrau, were delighted

Interior of St Stephen's, Vienna

that such an opportunity had offered itself.

Josef therefore went to Vienna. But he never forgot his first master: "I am," he said in later life, "grateful to this man, now in his grave, because he kept me occupied in so many directions."

2. *Imperial City*

VIENNA is one of the show-places of the world; one of the few truly international cities. It is beautiful today. To Josef Haydn, at the age of eight, it must have appeared as out of this world. Accustomed to the villages and tiny, intimate, towns of the Burgenland, it seemed vast. The more so because on every side new buildings of great splendour were springing up. For almost a hundred years a succession of Emperors—Leopold I, Joseph I, and Charles VI—had engaged architects of the stature of Johann Fischer von Erlach, Joseph Fischer von Erlach, and Johann von Hildebrandt, as well as numerous skilled Italians, to make a city worthy of an Empire. They engaged Italian, German, and Austrian sculptors and painters to beautify great new churches in the Baroque style—like the Church of St Charles—and such buildings as the Schwarzenburg Palace. But the great glory of Vienna was the Imperial Palace of Schönbrunn, in suburban Vienna, intended as a "summer residence" for the royal family, and laid around with gardens and parks exquisitely planned. This palace was still building when Josef Haydn arrived in Vienna and it was not ready for occupation until 1749.

One day in 1745 Haydn and his fellow choristers were commanded to perform at Schönbrunn. Finding free time on a summer's afternoon the choristers explored the mysteries of the scaffolding and scandalised the Court officials by playing noisy games high up on the walls of the building. Such was the disturbance that the Empress—

the beautiful Maria Theresa, who had come to the throne
in the year in which Haydn came to Vienna—pointed out
the ringleader and ordered him a beating. It was Josef
Haydn who came under the royal displeasure and the heavy
hand of Reutter, his choir-master. But the Empress had

The Great Gallery at Schönbrunn

her own troubles. Ever since her accession Frederick "the Great", of Prussia, had determined to reduce the importance and influence of Austria, and had thrown the whole of Europe into the turmoil of war.

At that time (but not later) Vienna itself remained free from military action, and within the city life went on—gay, uninhibited, and exciting. As a chorister Haydn spent much of his time in the Cathedral of St Stephen—which had been built in the twelfth century and of which the great tower dominated the centre of the city. He learned the richly varied music of the Church; the works of the great sixteenth-century masters, Palestrina (1525–94) and Lassus (1532–94), and those associated with Austria—including Jacob Handl (1550–91) and Heinrich Isaac (1450–1517); of Italian Baroque composers of whom the best-known in Vienna was Antonio Caldara (1670–1736); and of the principal Austrian composers of the day—Johann Fux (1660–1741), also a famous teacher, who was head of the Court music, and Reutter himself.

There was much other music. Plays with songs or instrumental pieces were arranged by the Jesuit fathers. Opera flourished, and so did oratorio. But there was a new emphasis on purely instrumental music and two Viennese composers in particular were busily refining the Italian-style opera overture into an independent symphony form. These composers were Georg Christoph Wagenseil (1715–77), and Georg Matthias Monn (1717–50), the one being music-master to the royal family and the other organist of St Charles' Church.

In 1745 Michael Haydn followed his elder brother into the choir of St Stephen's. Of the two he was probably the better singer; the beauty of his soprano voice was frequently

commended whereas that of Josef aroused no especial
comment. Certainly outside of musical studies Michael
was the more industrious and was well able to hold his
own with any boy of his age in classics, geography, or
history. Neither Josef nor Michael thought much of
Reutter as a teacher, for he was too occupied with his own
affairs to give more than casual attention to the needs of his
choristers. They were, therefore, thrown largely on their
own initiative. In a sense this was a good thing, for it
prevented the formation of a too narrow outlook. Living
in an atmosphere of music they could absorb it by ear.
However, both did their best to master the basic techniques
of musical composition, their regular guide being Fux's
famous instruction-book, *Gradus ad Parnassum* (*Steps to
Parnassus*). This work, containing the first principles of
combining individual melodic lines into the textures of
counterpoint, was known all over Europe, and in 1742
it had been translated into serviceable German by the
Leipzig scholar Lorenz Mizler (1711–78). Since Mizler was
a friend and former pupil of Johann Sebastian Bach and a
firm defender of the "scientific" principles of northern
German music, a link between north and south begins
to appear.

One of the most attractive characteristics of Josef Haydn,
as already noted, was his sense of humour. It was less
attractive to his superiors. One day in 1749, Haydn—whose
voice was breaking anyway—could no longer resist the
impulse to cut off one of the pigtails which the boy-
choristers of Vienna wore in those days. Reutter was not
amused. A firm believer in corporal punishment he offered
Haydn the alternative of a public beating or instant dis-
missal. The culprit, with memories of Reutter's efficiency

as executioner undimmed by the passage of time, chose expulsion as the less painful course. Michael remained behind to expunge this blot from the family name by such exemplary behaviour that, when his voice broke, he was kept on as assistant organist at St Stephen's.

Josef was, literally, out on the street, with nowhere to go and no prospects: a failure. The next ten years or so were desperately difficult as he tried to earn a living and at the same time to advance his ambition to be a composer. His parents, away in Rohrau, were deeply concerned, and, parent-like, urged him to take a safe job. They thought he would have made a good priest. Perhaps he would; but that was not his ambition.

Befriended by Johann Spangler—a tenor in the Choir of St Michael's Church in the city centre—who gave him lodging and helped him to get casual work as singer and violinist, and to find pupils, he just managed to make ends meet. But his private study had to be confined to the night hours, and then only when he was not out playing chamber or dance music. His next benefactor was Anton Buchholz, who offered him a generous loan of 150 gulden. (In his will Haydn remembered this by making provision for Buchholz's daughter, Anna.) As a composer, Haydn wrote his first setting of the Mass (a "short Mass" in F major), and various sets of pieces, collectively known as divertimentos, cassations, or nocturnes. These were useful for the musical evenings that were held in the wealthier households, and because they were expected to be of a genial character Haydn did not hesitate to introduce ideas from the popular music of the day.

In 1754 Anna Maria Haydn died. In that year Michael was away in the Hungarian part of the Empire, where he composed several Masses and established his credentials as a church musician. Three years later he was taken on as Music Director by Count Firmian, Bishop of Grosswardein in Pressburg (now Bratislava), whose uncle, Sigismund, was Archbishop of Salzburg. In 1762 Michael was invited to Salzburg as Music Director to the Archbishop in Salzburg, and there he remained for the rest of his life. Although not yet overshadowed by his elder brother he was denied the fame that might have come to him in Salzburg, because the six-year-old son of one of his Salzburg colleagues was attracting wider attention. This was Wolfgang Amadeus Mozart, already the musical wonder of Europe.

Still Josef Haydn plodded on. He made friends with an actress, who invited him to write a comic opera—*The Crooked Devil*—of which the music is lost. He became acquainted with the Court poet and opera librettist Pietro Metastasio (1698–1782), who recommended pupils to him. He met the Italian composer, singer, and singing-teacher Niccolò Porpora (1686–1766), who gave Haydn lessons in return for his acting as general factotum in his household. He also met Karl Ditters von Dittersdorf (1739–99), already a successful composer and a well-known violinist. By 1755 or so Haydn might be said to have been on the fringes of high society. That is to say, he was fairly frequently asked into the houses of the wealthy to give music lessons, or to take part in musical performances, and then sent downstairs to eat in the servants' quarters. There was, however, one nobleman who took a personal interest in him. This was Karl Joseph, Count von Fürnberg.

3. Director of Music

WHEN HAYDN WAS A YOUNG MAN music was not laid out in the categories that were established in his old age. There was church music and non-church music, it is true. But even here there was a border territory, on which divisions between sacred and secular were difficult to find if one did not follow the words too closely. Instrumental ensemble music was determined by occasion, and its requirements by the place of performance. In a small room it was only possible to use a handful of instruments. In a larger room, or in a theatre, more instruments were practicable. For out-of-doors occasions wind instruments were often in demand. Conditions, therefore, dictated some part of the nature of musical composition. Other conditions affected style—that is, the relationship between melody and harmony, and the structural design of pieces.

Haydn was born into an age in which melodic beauty, clarity of expression, and precision were being increasingly cultivated. An age also in which "sensibility" was regarded as a particular virtue. The Baroque style—by then thought to be "heavy"—was on its way out, although the great Baroque masters, Handel and Bach, were active right through Haydn's apprenticeship. The lighter, artificial (as it seems to us), rococo style was in. But the shepherds and shepherdesses of the rococo decorations in the great houses which Haydn visited were, during his lifetime, to give way to representations of real-life peasants. In paintings by some of the German artists contemporary with Haydn—

Josef Haydn

for instance, Friedrich Wilhelm Hirt, of Frankfurt, Johann Andreas Hurlein, of Fulda, or Joseph Steisser, of Munich— one may see the change taking place. The shepherds of

Arcady are replaced by peasants of Germany. In his last oratorio, *The Seasons* (1801), Haydn, in depicting country life, also reflected this change.

Haydn was one of those rare men who altered the whole quality of an art. This was because, through his intuition, he understood the direction in which feeling and not only art was moving. In this he was helped by his study of the forward-looking music of Carl Philipp Emanuel Bach (1714–88), whose keyboard sonatas were an inspiration to many. In Haydn's music we sense a development of power. Late works—particularly the last symphonies, *The Creation*, the final string quartets—are of an intensity not to be found in the early works.

But without the early works there would have been no late works. Now the early works came into being because Haydn tried to provide the kind of music that people wanted. Being poor, and relatively inconspicuous, he had to do so.

Count von Fürnberg, like every other Austrian count, had a house in Vienna and an estate in the country. His country seat was at Weinzierl on the Danube. Down there a good deal of music was practised. The Count liked music but was, apparently, unable to afford particularly good players. Chamber music was regularly provided by the castle caretaker, the local parson, a cellist whose name was Albrechtsberger, and—when he was free—Josef Haydn. Some of the music used at von Fürnberg's musical evenings is to be seen in the Music Department of the National Library in Budapest. It includes string quartets by Josef Haydn, some of those which belong to the set of six labelled Opus 2. (There had also been six quartets in Opus 1.) Of these, two had started life as divertimentos, with parts also for horns.

The string quartet—for 2 violins, viola, and 'cello—separated from other chamber music, which previously had always included harpsichord, almost by accident. Having discovered the possibilities of the medium Haydn went on to exploit them. But von Fürnberg also discovered possibilities in Josef Haydn. He spoke with a friend of his, Count Ferdinand Maximilian von Morzin, who was a Privy Councillor and Governor of a region of Bohemia (now in Czechoslovakia), and employed a private staff of musicians to help maintain his dignity. In 1760 Haydn was taken on his staff as Music Director (*Kapellmeister*). With 200 gulden a year as salary, free board and lodging, and free wine, he felt he had arrived. During the winter he worked in von Morzin's house in Vienna. In summer he transferred with his colleagues to the Castle of Lukaveč, near Pilsen, in Bohemia, where the country atmosphere was familiar and congenial to him. He composed divertimentos and symphonies, none of exceptional character but satisfactory to his employer.

At twenty-eight Haydn had written none of the works by which he became famous. He was one among many musicians busily pursuing the new symphonic style and encaged in the music-room of an obscure aristocrat whose means were unequal to his pretensions. Haydn did not stay long with von Morzin. First, he had married and found it expedient to try to better himself. Second, the Count found himself short of money, as a result of which, and to cause himself the least inconvenience, he dismissed his musicians. In fact, Haydn should not have married since his contract forbade it. Later on he wished that he had not, for the wife he married in 1760 eventually fell short of his expectations. She was Anna Maria Keller, daughter of a Viennese wig-maker.

Among the greater magnates of the Empire none was more important, or powerful, than Paul Anton Esterházy, Prince of Galanta. The territories of Esterház were widespread, stretching out into Hungary. The Prince's seat was in Eisenstadt (known by its Hungarian name as Kismarton, or St Martin's), an important town, with 2,500 inhabitants, in the heart of the Burgenland. In 1760 Prince Paul was on the look-out for a young man who could prepare himself to suceed the then Music Director (Gregorius Werner), at the castle at Eisenstadt. Favourably impressed by what he had heard of Josef Haydn he offered him the post of Deputy Music Director, with a salary twice that previously paid by von Morzin, and with more fringe benefits.

In the summer of 1761 Haydn and his wife arrived in Eisenstadt and settled in the apartment allocated to them in the barrack-like building, above the Castle, and near to the church in the Upper Town, set aside for the musicians. One disadvantage of the Haydns' lodging was that the rehearsal room was next door; but for Josef it meant that he did not have far to go to work. Anyway it was pleasant for him to live among his fellow-musicians, with whom he could discuss his ideas. One reason for Haydn's eminence as a composer was the fact that he was on good terms with his variously-gifted colleagues.

4. The New Appointment

HAYDN WAS HAPPY to be established in the Burgenland, over which his friends and relatives were scattered. The countryside, which he loved, was beautiful and there was plenty of opportunity for him to indulge in his favourite pleasures, of hunting and fishing, of visiting his gipsy friends—whose music he heard with delight and noted down for future reference, and of spending convivial evenings in the local inns. Haydn's favourite among these was the Angel—a charming building opened in 1711 and, like most of Eisenstadt, much as it was in Haydn's day. Here he met his colleagues off-duty, the local farmers, minor Court and town officials, and travellers on their way to and from Vienna. Of a conspicuously friendly and open nature, Haydn was popular. Speaking in the local dialect German, or in Croat, he was always good for lively anecdotes. Also he was generous of sympathy for those with problems or in distress.

To be the Deputy Music Director to a Prince, with the right to succession to the senior post in due course, was the height of Haydn's ambition insofar as official posts were concerned. He had justified himself in the eyes of his family, and his father was proud to be able to come over to visit his son at Eisenstadt. The old man did not have long to appreciate Josef's success, for in the late summer of 1763 he was injured by a fall of wood and his injuries proved fatal. On September 14 Matthias Haydn was buried at Rohrau. Josef went to the funeral and soon afterwards, characteristically, made over his own share in his father's estate to his younger brother Johann.

As a servant of an eighteenth-century prince, Haydn had to put up with various indignities. He was obliged by contract to wear the household uniform, to put on fancy dress for masquerades at the Castle, to "behave in a modest and restrained manner", to refrain from indelicate methods of eating and drinking, to wait on his employer morning and afternoon for his instructions, and to be punctual and obedient. He was required to control and discipline the musical staff (under the supervision of the ageing Werner), to teach the women singers, to look after music and instruments, and not to undertake outside commissions without permission. He was in charge of the chapel music, as well as of that for all entertainments, and had to be prepared to perform on those instruments on which he was expert. In the twentieth century such conditions would be thought intolerable. Haydn, however, was no rebel. That the power of a prince was absolute was an accepted part of his upbringing, and he saw no reason to think that the principle was improper. More and more people were coming to question this absolutism—as, for instance, Wolfgang Mozart in Salzburg—but not Haydn. He was a natural conservative, questioning the assumed privileges neither of the Catholic Church nor of the secular ruler. At the same time he was never prepared to lie down under injustice, whether to himself or his friends.

Appointed by Prince Paul Anton (who played the violin and the 'cello), Haydn soon had to adjust to a new employer. Paul Anton died in 1762, and was succeeded by his brother Nicholas. Prince Nicholas was all for splendour, and in his magnificence was the envy of every other Austrian aristo-

*A baryton
of Haydn's time*

crat. He was, however, personally modest, vivacious, and a notable lover of the arts. So far as music was concerned his favourite instrument was the baryton (a bass viol type of instrument, with six main strings but with 16 supplementary wire strings so placed that they could be plucked by the left thumb. The tone is quite enchanting.) For this instrument Haydn composed solos, duets, and concertos—

some 163 works in all—while he was obliged to include it in various divertimentos, trios, and so on. With Prince Nicholas he was on excellent terms, and as the years passed and Haydn's fame increased, the relationship between them grew more and more friendly. Prince Nicholas ruled for thirty years.

Haydn was a busy practical musician. His first duty was to provide music for all the occasions that demanded it. For dramatic performances, for balls, for private family pleasure, for formal occasions, for chapel services. If he could supplement the existing stock so much the better (a prince was pleased if his Kapellmeister was a competent composer, because the credit came back to him); but he was not in the first place required to be a specialist composer. Gregorius Werner, until he grew old and rather morose, was an efficient Director of Music. But he was not an outstanding composer. He was, in fact, quite an interesting composer, and the dramatic music which he wrote, based on peasant life and popular tunes, deserves its place in the annals of musical comedy. But outside of Vienna and Eisenstadt Werner's music was unfamiliar.

With Haydn it was otherwise. He came to Eisenstadt as a composer of some promise. When he arrived he discovered a talented team to work with. So, inspired by princely approval and friendly co-operation from the singers and players under him, he worked with a will. On May 17, 1762, Prince Nicholas made a ceremonial entry into Eisenstadt. Haydn enjoyed preparing the music for this occasion. Even more for the marriage festivities of Nicholas's son, Anton, to Maria Erdödy, at the end of the year. For this gave him a chance to compose an opera— a pastoral piece entitled *Acide e Galatea* (a well-known story

Prince Nicholas Esterházy at Eisenstadt

which had once inspired Handel to a serenata). The opera, gay with Italian-style melodies, pleased the performers as well as a distinguished audience of 600 who were packed into the great hall-cum-theatre of the Castle. But what Haydn most enjoyed writing at this time was symphonies. During his first five years of office at Eisenstadt he composed about 15 works of this nature. Increasingly they showed a feeling for expression and a felicity in handling the sounds of orchestral instruments that began to make some people aware of a new voice in music.

Of the early symphonies those that aroused most interest were those which were composed soon after his arrival in Eisenstadt, entitled "Le Matin" ("Morning"), "Le Midi" ("Afternoon"), and "Le Soir" ("Evening"). In these symphonies the range of keys is wider than was then customary, the length of melodic phrases is often more varied than the conventions of the period allowed, and the rhythms and instrumental colours suggest—as Haydn was so often to do—the vitality of life outside a castle music-room.

In "Le Midi" there is an important part for solo violin—written for Luigi Tomasini, the talented orchestral leader at Eisenstadt. How much Haydn felt indebted to Tomasini is shown in his remark that no one played his quartet music so well as this friendly Italian. In the third movement of "Le Midi" (a symphony with five movements, for as yet the regular four-movement form to be encountered in later Haydn, and in Mozart, was not established) there is also an important part for 'cello—originally for Joseph Weigl, another member of the band and also a close friend of the composer.

The resident staff of musicians at Eisenstadt, working under Haydn, included five violins, one 'cello, one double-bass, a flute, two oboes, two bassoons, two horns, two soprano singers, one alto, two tenors, a bass, and an organist. The wind-players were from time to time augmented from a group of military musicians (who also provided music for hunting parties), while most were able to double on another instrument than their own. It was also customary when advertising for servants to the Castle to give preference to those with musical ability.

As Haydn's success became more certain his musical superior, Werner—feeling that all his long years of service, and the 16 Masses he had composed, and of which he was so proud, went for nothing any longer—grew increasingly jealous. Not least because Haydn's salary, which had started at 600 gulden, by 1764 was standing at 782. His own remained frozen at 482 gulden. In his house outside the town Werner brooded over his misfortunes. At the beginning of 1766, aged seventy-one, he died, and was rewarded for his labours with a splendid funeral and an eloquent monument. Now in undisputed control of the Esterházy music Haydn decided to move out of the musicians' building. He bought a small house from widow Schleicher, just below the Castle Park, five minutes walk from the Castle itself, and in the other direction from the Franciscan Church, and two minutes from the Angel in the parallel main street of the town. Until her death, Mrs Schleicher lived on the ground floor of the house, the Haydns and any resident pupils on the first floor. Haydn paid for his house in instalments, and began to complain that because of his wife's bad housekeeping he was less well off than he should have been. Mrs Haydn, unable to have children, developed excessive religious enthusiasm, and some of the housekeeping money was diverted to religious charities, of which there were many.

By now Haydn had found a place for his brother Johann at the Castle. In 1764 he was taken on as an extra tenor in the chapel choir. In this capacity he was able to take part in the performance, in 1766, of Josef's first large-scale Mass: the so-called "Great Organ Mass".

5. *The Palace of Esterház*

IN THE EIGHTEENTH CENTURY, a prince, a duke, a count (Nicholas Esterházy carried all those titles), found it necessary to have at least two residences; one for the winter, one for the summer. In addition to a palace in Vienna and a castle in Eisenstadt the Esterházys had accumulated a number of other houses. But Nicholas decided that none was sufficiently commodious or magnificent to suit all his requirements. He inspected the hunting-lodge at Süttör, a Hungarian town on the southern shores of Neusiedler Lake, and planned to replace it with a palace that should rival those at Versailles and Schönbrunn. The new palace was built and when completed was breathtaking. The French Ambassador said that it was the only place in Europe to rival the royal palace in Versailles. The cost of the building was ten million gulden.

The Prince set out to make his new palace a great centre of culture. Innumerable artists and sculptors were employed to beautify it, and within the grounds an opera-house and a marionette theatre were built.

From 1766 Haydn was often required to transfer to Esterház, as, of course, were all his colleagues. So far as working conditions were concerned, Haydn had no objection to going there. He loved the opera-house and, even more, the marionette theatre. But the living conditions were far from ideal. As at Eisenstadt, there was a separate building—with 54 rooms—for the music staff. In general, each musician was allowed two rooms in which to

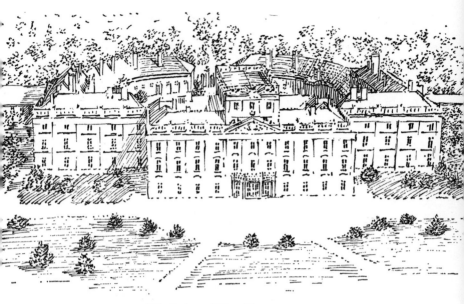

The Palace of Esterház

live with his family. Haydn was favoured by having three rooms at his disposal. The conditions were cramped, and living one on top of the other caused quarrels to arise.

In 1772, the Prince, disturbed that discord should reign where harmony should prevail, gave orders that musicians should no longer be permitted to bring their wives and families to Esterház. The only exceptions to this rule were Haydn, Tomasini, and two singers. In modern times, employees so treated would go on strike. In the eighteenth century the practice of striking had not been established. But under Haydn's guidance the next best protest was staged—a walk-out.

One of Haydn's most famous works is the "Farewell" Symphony. The circumstances of its composition should not be allowed to obscure the fact that it is a fine symphony, in which a variety of moods are portrayed. In the opening

movement there is even a tragic note, recalling the solemn
music of two symphonies composed during the same period,
that in F minor known as "La Passione" because it was
performed during Passiontide, and that in E minor, known
as the "Mourning" Symphony. In the second, minuet,
movement of this symphony, Haydn indicates the appro-
priate mood in two ways. First, by the use of minor tonality;
second, by canonic procedure.

(Ex.1)

(*imitation in canon, one octave lower*)

The "Farewell" Symphony is remarkable for its last
movement, which falls into two sections. The first of these
is a sonata-style *presto* which leads into a contrasting *adagio*.
This moves from the key of A major to that of F sharp
major, in which the instruments disappear from the score
one by one until only two violins are left. At its first
performance, before the Prince and his guests, the musicians
put out their candles and left the orchestra as they came to
the end of their parts. Prince Nicholas appreciated that this
was a gesture of protest. It was too bad that the orchestral
players should be denied their family life for so long.
He, therefore, gave orders that the Court should pack up
and return to Eisenstadt.

At this time Haydn had worries enough of his own. In
1768 half the town of Eisenstadt was severely damaged by

fire. Haydn's house, and with it a number of his compositions, including opera scores, was destroyed. In those days this kind of "ordeal by fire" was common, and the subject, not in itself in any way humorous, is treated by Haydn in a comic opera of about this time. *Die Feuersbrunst* (*The Conflagration*) is a light-hearted picture of the small-town life that Haydn knew so well. The characters include the traditional comic "Hanswirst" (in this case, a chimney sweep), a steward of a large estate, his daughter, an innkeeper, a priest—and so on. Haydn did not take this task too seriously, and the first two movements of the introductory *sinfonia* were written by his pupil, Ignaz Pleyel (1757–1831), while the third was borrowed from his own opera *L'infedeltà delusa* (see p. 45). But there are moments of powerful musical commentary—as when the house catches fire:

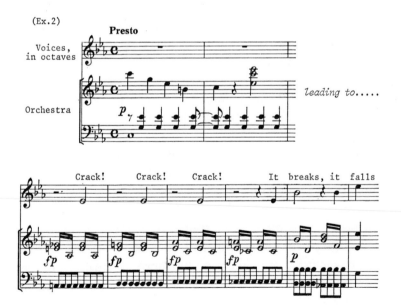

Although the cost of the rebuilding of his house was borne by Prince Nicholas, Haydn's resources were so severely strained that he had to submit to the indignity of applying to the Town Council for relief from taxation. For some years he was given remission from the "military tax", payable through the town to the royal revenues. A succession of wars, culminating in the Seven Years War that ended in 1763, and persistent unease in Europe entailed the maintenance of a large standing army in the Austrian dominions, the greater part of the cost of which was borne by the ordinary citizens.

Haydn was also engaged in a running battle with his neighbours on either side, and in repairing the damage caused by his wife's incautious tongue. More and more Mrs Haydn—who used on occasion to roll her pastry on her husband's manuscripts—became a trial. As he said, Haydn had his "private cross" to bear. Despite, or because of this, his art matured during the early Esterház years. Apart from the works already named, his output included a number of comic operas which faithfully reproduced the expected clichés of *opera buffa* style, the St Cecilia and St Nicholas Masses, the string quartets of Op. 9, Op. 17, and Op. 20, a number of pianoforte sonatas, as well as many minor works.

A great composer has a distinctive style. But his individuality consists of his appreciation of many different modes of expression. Haydn was at home with Italian music, which dominated the opera-houses of Europe. The melodic ease of the *bel canto* style is to be found in his operas and Masses alike. He was also at home with the sterner, more scientific principles, of northern Germany. And he intuitively perceived that in the folk-music of his Burgen-

The Opera House at Esterház

land friends and in the music of the gipsies there was a particular virtue which could be introduced into the broad tradition of music. Haydn was a born musical conversationalist. Within the sonata-style that had assumed importance during his youth, he amplified the development of melodic material. In the string quartet he understood that a proper balance depended on the independence of the four instruments. So far as the keyboard sonata was concerned he followed the lead of C. P. E. Bach, who was the musician who did most, by his playing as much as by his compositions, to make the pianoforte the expressive medium it was to become.

(Ex.3)

A work of this period which shows the many-sidedness of the mature Haydn is the Quartet in F minor (Op. 20, No. 5), with its taut opening movement—with marvellous and mystical changes of chordal colour towards the end; a sturdy and uncourtly minuet—with unconventional balance of phrase units; a serene slow movement—the only one in this work in the major key; and a final fugue built on two themes. The upper theme in the example given above had been used by many composers during the Baroque period.

Since his earliest years, Haydn had been in the habit of using contrapuntal devices—of canon, of fugue—in his symphonies and quartets. Anywhere else than at Eisenstadt or Esterház they would have been dismissed as "too heavy", or too old-fashioned. It was fortunate that Prince Nicholas knew that while he was entitled to give instructions concerning his Music Director's table manners, he was not entitled to tell him how to compose. He really was rather proud of Haydn's talents.

6. *The Empress*

THOSE WHO ARE GREAT in the eyes of the world are never reluctant to court the favour of those who are greater. Prince Nicholas had built his Palace at Esterház with the intention of lodging crowned heads there. On September 1 and 2, 1773, his outlay appeared to pay its proper dividends. For on those days the Empress Maria Theresa, who was also Queen of Hungary, with the Princesses Anna and Elisabeth, and Prince Maximilian, were his guests. In the Hungarian part of her dominions the Empress was especially popular and so when she came to Esterház, by way of Ödenburg (where her host met her), the inhabitants were delighted. Truly the grounds of the Palace looked magnificent, lit with thousands of lanterns which brought the splendid statuary to life and made the carefully tended flower-beds glow with colour. And when fireworks were sent into the sky, fitfully illuminating the façade of the Palace, 8,000 spectators cheered their appreciation of them, and of the Empress, and of their Prince.

For Josef Haydn it was a busy time. In the banqueting-hall musicians were in attendance. For the salon orchestral music was laid on. The Empress paid a visit to the opera-house, and she also went to a performance in the marionette theatre. The symphony in C major (No. 48), known by the name of the Empress, was composed in honour of this occasion. Especially in the finale the brilliant scene is re-captured in a vivacious musical statement which shows how

44

the composer could bring to life what is no more than the familiar scale of C major.

The comic opera *L'infedeltà delusa*, a brilliant transposition of Neapolitan *opera buffa* into an Austro-Hungarian musical dialect (for Haydn's robustness, as well as his more tender qualities, are in evidence), was put on for Maria Theresa on her first night at Esterház. The cast and the orchestra were well prepared, for they had performed this opera during the summer for the Prince's widowed sister-in-law. But it was the marionette opera, *Philemon and Baucis*, given its first performance on the second night of the Empress's visit, that captured everybody's fancy. It was beautifully and imaginatively set, with backcloths showing every conceivable scene, and in the final set the castle park appeared—as background to the Imperial Habsburg coat of arms. Haydn was presented to the Empress who, when reminded that she had once been the cause of his being beaten, pointed out that her former severity had been justified. "If I want to hear a good opera," she said afterwards, "I go to Esterház". In 1777 she borrowed Haydn and his team to perform at celebrations in Vienna in honour of the Archduchess Christine.

Somewhat to his surprise, Haydn found himself becoming well-known in Vienna. At times, although he loved the environment, he felt isolated at Eisenstadt and at Esterház. He was bothered with trivialities—a continuing law-suit with one of his disagreeable neighbours in Eisenstadt over a party-wall, his wife's indiscretions which increased as time went on, the troubles of his numerous relatives, and the problems of his subordinates. He had a frequent urge to travel, especially to Italy. But the Prince was always unwilling to let him out of his sight. However, in the heart

The banqueting hall at Eisenstadt, now known as the Haydn room

of his native province, drawing on the inspiration of life around him, his powers increased. And so did his reputation. Orchestral players came and went, and when they went they took works of Haydn with them. Visiting virtuosi were often employed at Eisenstadt and Esterház, and they, too, carried the fame of the Music Director abroad. For instance, Andreas Lidl, the baryton player, gave performances of Haydn's music in London and Oxford in the 1770s, while further news of Haydn was surely taken back to England by the English singer Jenny Barton, who took part in performances at Esterház in 1778.

Haydn's works were published (usually without his

knowledge or permission) in Germany, Holland, France, and England. The musical authorities in Vienna began to wake up to the distinguished composer living out in the country, and in 1775, he was commissioned to write an oratorio, *Il ritorno di Tobia*, for a charity performance of the Society of Musicians. A year later he was asked to write an opera for the Court. Unfortunately in Vienna, as in the Court operas in other places in Germany and Austria, a "closed shop" principle was worked. For the most part Italian musicians were in charge, and whenever it was possible to impede a non-Italian composer, they did so with some malice. Haydn—like Mozart, Mendelssohn, Spohr, Wagner, and many others—found the Italians very trying and obstructive. The opera, *La vera constanza* (*True constancy*), which he got to rehearsal stage in Vienna, he withdrew. Fortunately, there was always the opportunity of performance at Esterház. In 1779, Haydn performed two of his operas there: *L'isola disabitata* (*The deserted island*), written to a libretto by Metastasio in honour of the Princess's birthday, and *La vera costanza*. Because the theatre had been damaged by fire Haydn found it necessary to restrict himself in the former. There were only one set and four characters. In *La vera costanza* the composer was handicapped by an indifferent libretto. So it is that in both works the level of achievement is uneven.

Just at this time Haydn let himself in for another complication. This began with the engagement of an Italian violinist, Antonio Polzelli, and his nineteen-year-old wife, Luigia—a soprano. Not really up to standard, according to the critical Prince, Luigia was handed over to the Director of Music with instructions that he should give her extra tuition.

Haydn, as he was the first cheerfully to admit, had had numerous affairs with women. He never understood why. He was, he pointed out, distinctly unhandsome—with a brown face (the result of gipsy blood or a liver complaint?), with ugly marks left by smallpox, and a growth on his nose that led him to the monastic doctors at Eisenstadt on the frequent occasions when it caused pain. He was not noticeably intellectual, and his conversation was earthy. But he had a remarkable fund of sympathy, and that, no doubt, was what made Luigia Polzelli pour out her soul to him. He promptly fell in love with her. This was an embarrassment, since she was so indifferent as a singer that the Prince would have dismissed her, except Haydn intervened on her behalf. It was a further embarrassment in that she was never satisfied. If Haydn gave her one gift she wanted two. Quite often, as with a valuable harpsichord which Haydn once gave her, she would sell his presents. The relationship persisted for years. In 1783, a son was born to Luigia. Ill-natured persons suggested that Haydn was his father. However this may have been, the boy was brought up in Haydn's house—as one among several pupils. Which goes to show how long-suffering Mrs Haydn was.

7. The Haydns and the Mozarts

WHILE JOSEF HAYDN was more and more coming into the limelight his brother, Michael, was pursuing his own course on the other side of Austria, in Salzburg. Having married Maria Magdalena Lipp, a Court singer and daughter of the Court organist, and enjoying a comfortable annual stipend of 300 florins (which was doubled in 1803 by the Archduke Ferdinand), he felt settled in Salzburg for life. He was not only Music Director there, but also organist of several churches, and the most reliable composer on the Archbishop's staff. He was sometimes the worse for drink, but never so seriously that he was unable to fulfil his duties, and his "peasant" manners offended the politer Salzburgers. He was, indeed, a voluminous composer. In the course of his life he wrote 52 symphonies, as well as concertos, serenades, cassations, divertimentos, nocturnes, and dances; and 26 Masses (two of them Requiems), and more than 300 other pieces of church music. Josef Haydn had the highest regard for his brother's skill in this department, and considered himself Michael's inferior. In truth, Michael covered a wide field as is shown on the one hand by an *Ave Regina* of 1770, which recalls the musical style of the great polyphonic era, and on the other by a splendid psalm-setting of 1788. (Ex. 4 and 5, p. 50).

After his death, Franz Schubert wrote of Michael's "tranquil and clear spirit". This is the quality that shines

(Ex.4)

(Ex.5)

*after 9 bars
change to
dominant key
of F major*

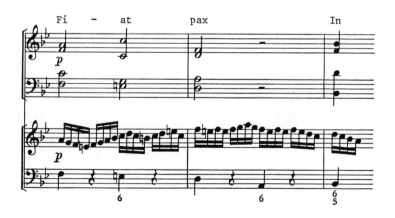

through his music. It is interesting to speculate as to what would have happened had Michael and Josef changed places. There is no doubt that the Esterházy family were more keenly interested in music than the Archbishop of Salzburg, so Josef's talent benefited from his environment more than did Michael's.

In Salzburg, one of Michael's colleagues was the violinist Leopold Mozart, who had a high opinion of his music. So it was that as he grew up, Wolfgang Mozart frequently had the excellent qualities of Haydn pointed out to him. Especially his mastery of counterpoint. At the beginning of November, 1773, Leopold Mozart wrote to his son—then in Mannheim—praising the "Hieronymus" Mass, and the motet (more truly a cantata) *Timete Dominum* (*Fear the Lord*)—which had been performed in the Cathedral on All Saints' Day. He drew particular attention to Michael's skill in rounding off the motet with a fugal "Alleluia". Leopold Mozart's enthusiasm was not misplaced. The way in which Haydn manages to make a glorious finale out of a basic four-note pattern (Ex. 6) is, indeed, remarkable.

(Ex.6)

This somewhat anticipates the way in which Wolfgang Mozart builds the figure in Ex. 7 into the last movement

(Ex.7)

of the "Jupiter" Symphony.

The younger Mozart also admired Michael's robust pieces, among which a Turkish March, with much percussion in the score, demonstrates not only this robustness, but also a general desire to look to distant parts for more exotic musical effects.

(Ex.8)

(scored for 2 trumpets, 2 horns, 2 bassoons, 2 oboes, 2 clarinets, cymbals, timpani, bass drum)

In 1783, the Salzburgers heard a symphony in E flat by Michael Haydn, which some may have remembered when, in later years, they listened to the great symphony (No. 39) in the same key by Mozart. This was how Haydn began his symphony:

(Ex.9)

After the movement which opens with this bold idea, there follow a slow movement, which is similar in feeling to many by John Christian Bach (1735–82), and a concluding *presto* which has something of the spirit of Josef Haydn.

From Mozart's point of view the only disadvantage was that Michael Haydn was a predictable composer. One knew the sort of thing he was likely to do next. Or rather, one knew what he would *not* do. Harmonically he was content to overwork the simplest formulas. This was very far from being the case with Josef Haydn, to whose music Mozart warmed more and more.

In the spring of 1781 Mozart resigned his office as Court organist in Salzburg, and, disillusioned by the treatment he had received from the Archbishop, left the city for Vienna. Later that year Haydn went up to Vienna—there being at the time great celebrations for a royal wedding—and heard some of his newly published quartets played. These quartets, Op. 33, were known as the "Russian" Quartets, being dedicated to the Grand Duke Paul of Russia. The quartets of Op. 33—the first works of this kind to have been composed by Haydn for ten years—made a deep impression on Mozart—who made his first acquaintance with the older composer during this time, and soon afterwards he wrote the first of the set of six quartets which he published in 1785 with a dedication to Josef Haydn. In 1784 Haydn and Mozart were much together and they both enjoyed the company of the British artistes Michael Kelly, and Stephen and Nancy Storace, who were in Vienna during that period. Years later Kelly recalled how he was once present at a musical evening at Storace's lodging, at which string quartets were played by Haydn, Karl Ditters von Dittersdorf (violins), Mozart (viola), and Johann Baptist

Wanhal (1739–1813). Wanhal was also a composer, industrious, popular, but not greatly talented. Kelly was so taken with Haydn that he went down to visit him in Eisenstadt, of which visit he wrote a delightful account in his *Reminiscences* (1816).

It was about this time that definite suggestions that Haydn should visit England began to be made. Overtures came from Lord Abingdon, an interesting, way-out, aristocrat, who scandalised his fellow peers by his radical views, and also by his competence as a composer. He was a strong supporter of the concerts organised in London by John Christian Bach, who had endeared himself to Mozart by his kindness to him in London many years before. But however much Haydn might wish to travel he had the permanent difficulty of getting away from Eisenstadt or Esterház. It was difficult enough even finding opportunity to spend as much time as he now found desirable in Vienna.

In 1780 Haydn began a business arrangement with the Viennese publishing house of Artaria, the owners of which realised that Haydn's music was likely to prove a profitable investment.

And again in the following year the London publisher William Forster came to the same conclusion. By no means displeased at such encouragement Haydn did, as he thought, the best for himself by selling certain works to both houses, to the temporary consternation of both. In those days, however, the odds were heavily weighted against a composer—there being no "performing rights" nor royalty payments as there are today—and it was a case of each man for himself. Among the works which Haydn sold, both to Artaria and Forster, was the set of instrumental pieces commissioned for the Good Friday devotions at

Cadiz Cathedral, and known as *The Seven Words of the Saviour on the Cross*.

It was in 1785 that Haydn met Leopold Mozart and after hearing the last three of the quartets that Wolfgang had dedicated to him said to Leopold that his son was the greatest composer he knew. Among creative artists Haydn was that very rare case: a man who was without jealousy or envy, and able freely to acknowledge genius in others. What is more, he was ready to learn from Mozart, as Mozart from him. From now on Haydn's instrumentation took on a higher degree of brilliance, his harmonies more subtlety; both came from a close study of Mozart's methods. Mozart, for his part, assimilated something of Haydn's sense of power and seriousness. In imitation of Haydn he began to preface the first movements of his symphonies with slow, often solemn, introductions. Other composers noted the manner in which Haydn was increasing the importance of symphonic music, and away in Bücke-burg, near Hanover, another of Sebastian Bach's sons, Johann Christoph Friedrich, was busy bringing his symphonic manner into line with that of Haydn. The most important of the symphonies composed by Haydn at this time are in the collection of six that were commissioned by a concert-going organisation in Paris. Among these are those nicknamed as "L'Ours" ("the Bear"), "La Poule" ("the Hen"), and "La Reine" ("the Queen").

8. *The Last Years of Prince Nicholas*

WHEN HE WAS AT HOME Haydn had an almost full-time job in looking after the interests of his relatives, his friends, his god-children—and Luigia Polzelli. He was also troubled by increasing deterioration in the health of his wife. Devoted to his family as he was—as many as could assembled at the tiny walled town of Bruck, between Eisenstadt and Rohrau, for an annual get-together—he found many calls on his time. By now he had nephews and nieces spread out all over the Burgenland and into Hungary, some prosperously married, some not so. His favourite sister Anna Maria (who married a local farrier named Frölich—the name of the present landlord of the Angel inn in Eisenstadt) had had fifteen children. Of these one, Anna Katharina, who married first a minor official at Eisenstadt Castle, and then, after his death, a shoemaker, was always in a bad way financially. Much of Haydn's generosity was invoked, and time after time he rescued her from improvidence and poverty. His reward came when in due course one of Anna Katharina's daughters devoted herself to looking after him in his last years. Then there was his brother Johann, a perpetual cause of anxiety, whose troubles Haydn heard and eased.

But the calls on his time from the Prince were many. In the opera-house at Esterház alone there was an annual repertory of opera to be prepared. Often he added arias to work by other composers—the Italians Pasquale Anfossi (1727–97), Giuseppe Sarti (1729–1802), and Domenico Cimarosa (1749–1801), being among the most popular. The only opera of his own composed towards the end of the rule of Prince Nicholas was *Armida*—an "heroic" opera in the manner of the traditional *opera seria*. The truth was that Haydn had begun to doubt his capacity as an opera composer. He knew what Mozart could accomplish, and that in this field he could not compete. In 1790 he intended performing *The Marriage of Figaro*, but this intention he was not to see fulfilled.

In 1787 Haydn published another famous set of quartets (Op. 50), which were dedicated to King Friedrich Wilhelm of Prussia. In the year following he composed three fine symphonies (Nos. 90, 91, and 92) for a French count. These symphonies, respectively in C major, E flat major, and G major, combine warmth of expression with a fine appreciation of contrapuntal movement, together with an increasing awareness of the possibilities inherent in un-expected changes of tonal centre (modulations).

It was in the next year that Haydn woke up one day to find an English visitor at the door of the musicians' building, in Eisenstadt, waiting to be let in. This was John Bland, the London publisher, who had been asked by Johann Peter Salomon (1745–1815), a German violinist now active in London concert promotion, to try to persuade Haydn to come to London. The answer was as always: it was not possible on account of the Prince. Bland, how-ever, did well out of the visit. Haydn, dissatisfied with the razor with which he was shaving himself at the time of Bland's arrival, said that he would give his best quartet for a decent razor. Bland promptly gave him his own, and

Haydn's garden house at Eisenstadt

took away the score of a newly written quartet—that in F minor-major, Op. 55, No. 2—which thereafter was known as the "Razor" Quartet.

On February 23, 1790, the wife of Prince Nicholas died. In September the Prince died in Vienna at the age of seventy-six. His body was brought back to Eisenstadt and laid with those of other members of the Esterházy family in the crypt of the Franciscan Church. Much as he lamented the death of his old patron, Haydn at last felt free. Particularly since the successor to the title, Nicholas's son Anton, caring little for music, reduced the strength of the music staff, and put Haydn almost into half-retirement. Having a pension of 1,000 florins a year from the will of Prince Nicholas, and his regular salary as well, he felt relatively well off. He could now consider a new life. The first thing to do was to go back to Vienna. In 1778 Haydn had sold his Eisenstadt home to the Court accountant, and since that time had been living in the musicians' building. Vacating his quarters there was, therefore, a relatively simple matter. He took temporary lodgings in Vienna until he should find a suitable house. But before he could get round to this there came an urgent invitation, which he had no longer to refuse.

9. *Universal Fame*

FOR THE SECOND TIME an unexpected visitor from London called on Haydn. This time, in 1790, it was Johann Peter Salomon. He got down to business at once, saying, "I am Salomon from London, and have come to take you back with me. We start tomorrow". First of all, however, Haydn had to obtain formal permission from Prince Anton, and also from the King of Naples, to whom he had promised a visit. This was rather more difficult, but since Haydn said that he would honour that engagement on his return, the King gave consent for a deferment. Before leaving Haydn said goodbye to Mozart, whose poignant words to his old friend were, "I fear, Papa, this is our last farewell". While Haydn was away in London Mozart died, on December 4/5, 1791.

Haydn and Salomon travelled by way of Munich, Bonn, Brussels, and Calais. In Bonn, where Ludwig van Beethoven was at that time deputy organist in the Elector's Chapel and where Salomon had been born and brought up, Haydn was greeted by the Elector himself, and in the chapel he heard a performance of one of his Masses. Once in London, where he stayed a day or two with Bland, of "Razor Quartet" fame, Haydn found his time fully occupied with a busy social programme as well as the obligations imposed on him by his contract with Salomon. This was handsome, being worth 5,000 gulden.

On March 11, 1791, the great day came when Haydn was to introduce the first of his so-called "London" Symphonies

—of which in the end there were twelve, spread over two visits and composed between 1791 and 1794. That which was played at Haydn's first London concert, in the Hanover Square Rooms, was No. 96 in D major. The orchestral players took to Haydn. They respected his practical competence as orchestral director (conducting was still done from the keyboard), and found him agreeable and unfussed. He used few words (possessing at that time only a very meagre store of English vocabulary), but was decisive and helpful with his gestures. Which was as well, since—unlike in Eisenstadt or Esterház—the professional musicians of London, making their livings by undertaking as much free-lance work as possible, were not much available for rehearsal. However, all went well, and the symphony was greatly appreciated; the slow movement, in fact, was encored.

Haydn appeared at numerous concerts during the season, and at performances at the Pleasure Gardens when the season was ended. He heard a great Handel Festival at Westminster Abbey, and was greatly impressed by the splendour of Handel's music. He went to Oxford, conducting the so-called "Oxford" Symphony (No. 92)—which had, in fact, been composed prior to his departure from Austria for another purpose—and receiving an honorary Doctor's degree. Of this he was very proud and afterwards frequently signed himself as "Doctor at Oxfort". He also visited Cambridge, and made other excursions into the country. A feeling of homesickness—which he expressed in letters to his friend Mrs von Genzinger (wife of a doctor in Vienna)—was relieved occasionally by meeting with old friends—like the Storaces whom he had known in Vienna, or expatriates, like William Cramer, among the professionals resident in London, or less permanent residents from abroad, like Jan Ladislav Dušek (1761–1812), a celebrated Bohemian pianist and composer, and his own one-time pupil Ignaz Pleyel. Pleyel had been brought to London to appear at the Professional Concerts which ran in rivalry with those organised by Salomon. Haydn's symphonies were also played at these concerts, which were directed by Cramer.

Sometimes, on the other hand, Haydn felt quite pleased not to be at home. As for instance when Luigia Polzelli's husband died, leaving her even more free to pursue her interest in the great composer. While in England he made up for the absence of his regular female companions by cultivating the society of Mrs Schroeter, widow of Johann Samuel Schroeter, who had succeeded J. C. Bach as Queen Charlotte's music-master, and Mrs Anne Hunter, wife of Dr John Hunter. Dr Hunter, a celebrated surgeon, proposed to Haydn that he should operate on the troublesome growth on Haydn's nose—a proposal that filled him with horror. He preferred to remain with his trouble rather than to submit to surgery.

Towards the end of his London visit Haydn had the unusual experience for an eighteenth-century European composer of encountering the music of Purcell. At one concert he accompanied the famous German singer Gertrud Mara in a performance of Purcell's song "From rosy bowers". He also heard the annual service of the "Charity Children" at St Paul's Cathedral, and found opportunity to visit Windsor Castle.

Haydn was a great success in England, and the lead in singing his praise was taken by Lord Abingdon, Dr Charles Burney, and William Shield, while amateur musicians clamoured for opportunity to play his symphonies at their music clubs, even in simplified arrangements. On excellent terms with the British Royal Family, Haydn attended a garden party given by the Duchess of York, at the end of June, 1792, and took his leave. He was due in Frankfurt to meet Anton Esterházy, who was there for the Coronation of Francis II as Emperor. On the way down the Rhine Haydn once more stopped off in Bonn, where he was entertained again by the Elector's musicians and asked for his advice by the young Beethoven.

During Haydn's long absence in England his wife had found a house in Gumpendorf (then, but no longer, a suburb of Vienna), in the parish of Mariahilf. This house, larger than that at Eisenstadt, is also now a museum. It was, however, some time before the Haydns could take possession. Substantial repairs were necessary and what with the slowness of the City Council in approving the alterations and of the workmen, it was not until 1797 that the new owners could move in.

In the meantime much had happened. Beethoven had moved to Vienna and placed himself under Haydn's tuition —which he did not find entirely fitting to his case. Apart from Beethoven's general conviction that his own talents were of a superior order, and his generally stubborn nature, there was, of course, what is now termed the generation gap. Haydn became venerable when comparatively young. The nickname "Papa" had dogged him long before he was sixty. Past his sixtieth birthday, he was really beginning to show his age. It was the same with his brother Michael. Now one of the older citizens of Salzburg he began to discover that his attitudes were different from those of the young. Among his pupils was Carl Maria von Weber

(1786–1826), whose father settled in Salzburg for a short time with the company of actors he directed. But the young Weber—even though Michael Haydn had offered to teach him free—did not recall his lessons with enthusiasm.

Contrary to outward appearances Josef Haydn, however, was very far from being a prisoner of his years. Indeed, the majority of the works by which he is generally known at the present time were composed in the last fifteen years or so of his life. The list is a formidable one.

10. *The Creation*

HAYDN RETURNED to England at the beginning of February 1794, and stayed there until the late summer of the next year. He was a most popular visitor, not least on account of his imperfect mastery of the English language. Concerning this there is an anecdote in a letter (November 22, 1828) from C. J. Latrobe to Charles Burney. (Latrobe was brother of Benjamin Latrobe, the famous American classical architect.) Haydn called at Latrobe's London home one day:

> When he entered the room, he found my wife alone, and as she could not speak German, and he had scarcely picked up a few English words, both were at a loss what to say. He bowed with foreign formality, and the following short explanation took place:
>
> H. "Dis Mr Latrobe's house?" The answer was in the affirmative.
>
> H. "Be you his Woman?" [meaning his wife.] "I am Mrs Latrobe," was the reply.
>
> After some pause, he looked round the room and saw his picture, to which he immediately pointed, and exclaimed, "Dat is me. I am Haydn".

As before Haydn was under contract to Salomon to direct concerts. Symphonies 100, in G major, and 101, in D minor-major—the "Military" and the "Clock"—were given their first performances. As had been a frequent practice when Haydn was previously in London the slow movements more often than not were encored. That of the

"Clock", with its combination of humour and beauty, asks for it!

(Ex.10)

Some of Haydn's latest string quartets were also played at the Salomon Concerts. During the summer he extended his knowledge of England further by travelling to the south and west, visiting the Isle of Wight, Winchester, Bath, and Bristol. Next winter Salomon was unable to continue his series of concerts, but Haydn was invited to participate in those organised by the violinist Giovanni Battista Viotti (1753–1824) at the King's Theatre, in the Haymarket. For those he composed the last three of his symphonies, No. 102, in B flat major; No. 103 in E flat major—the "Drum roll"; and No. 104, in D minor-major—the "London".

It was suggested to Haydn by Queen Charlotte—who had herself been a pupil of J. C. Bach—that he should make his home in England. But he was still a servant of the Prince of Esterházy. A few days after Haydn left Austria in 1794, Prince Anton died, and was succeeded by Nicholas II. Unlike his father, this Prince was concerned that the music of his Court should be taken seriously, and he indicated to Haydn that he should come home and set about rebuilding the orchestra.

Haydn returned to Austria to find himself treated with a much greater respect—on account of his successful forays into England. His symphonies had become extremely popular in Vienna, and pride of place went to the "Surprise", the slow movement of which is still the most successful of musical "jokes", because the humour is of the simplest and most obvious kind, albeit enclosed within a movement which has a charm that is greater than the element of humour. What touched Haydn most at this time, however, was the honour paid to him by Count von Harrach, who had erected a statue, in commemoration of the glory its most famous son had brought to the village, in the park of the castle in Rohrau.

Nicholas II did not use Esterház any more and the Court alternated between Vienna in winter and Eisenstadt in summer. There were other changes too. The Prince's taste in music lay in the direction of church music. Once a year, for his birthday, he therefore expected his Director of Music to produce a Mass. Between 1796 and 1802 Haydn composed six Masses. Different in temper from those of his earlier years these were distinguished by the breadth of their ideas, their reflection of the state of the world, and the significance and variety of their orchestration.

Europe was convulsed by the Napoleonic Wars, and the anxieties of the times are particularly echoed in the Mass, composed in 1796, which Haydn entitled "In time of war", and in which he gave especial prominence to the drums. In this, as in many of his later works, dramatic contrasts of rhythm, harmony, and instrumentation anticipate the manner of expression of Beethoven. The Mass in D minor is known as the "Nelson" Mass, because Lord Nelson heard it performed in Eisenstadt in 1800.

Haydn's Masses (and the *Te Deum* of 1800) are a glorious recapitulation of the southern European tradition of Catholic church music; vibrant, uninhibited, marvellously direct in expression. Haydn's religious faith was simple, but an inspiration to him. It filled him with a great sense of joy, and because this was reflected in his church music there were those in former times who did not appreciate the quality of his religious outlook, and complained that the music was too cheerful. At the same time they overlooked the compassion that is also to be found in this music; such compassion as is to be found, for example, in these bars of the *Te Deum* of 1800.

san-gui-ne re-de-mi- -sti

Haydn's music is to be ranked as among the most signifi-
cant ever composed in Europe. It carried the impulses of
the sixteenth century (in the Masses note the strict canon
of the opening of the Credo of the "Nelson" Mass); of the
school of Bach, in contrapuntal procedures that had been
often disregarded since Bach's time; of Italian opera and
church music; of the expressive keyboard music of Emanuel
Bach; of the logical sonata tradition as developed in Italy,
Austria, and Germany; and also of the English choral
tradition. Haydn brought all these impulses together, and
interlaced them with memories of the folk music of the
Danube basin, and of the gipsies. He was at heart always a
native of the Burgenland. But he moved among crowned
heads. He had the power to unite ideas that were aristo-
cratic with those that were democratic. Like Handel whose
oratorios impressed him so much in England, he became a
universal composer in his lifetime.

In 1797 Haydn settled in his new house in Vienna. In
England he had admired the words and music of "God
save the King". Because of the wars which Napoleon had
unleashed in Europe, patriotism was in the ascendant.
In Austria a competition to provide words for a national
anthem was held. The winner was Lorenz Leopold Haschka,
whose poem "Gott erhalte Franz den Kaiser" ("God sustain
Emperor Franz") was set to music by Haydn and performed
in the Court Theatre in Vienna for the first time on Feb-

ruary 12, 1797, the birthday of Franz Joseph I. The melody (which Haydn used as a theme for a set of variations in the so-called "Emperor" Quartet—Op. 76, No. 3) caught on immediately. In due course it was sung all over Europe and America. In Germany it was adopted as a national hymn, in Britain and America it was used in hymn-books. In its original form the music of the "Emperor's Hymn" appeared as follows:

(Ex.12)

The oratorios of Handel inspired Haydn to consider the composition of an oratorio in similar style. Handel himself had more than once thought of John Milton's *Paradise Lost* as a fitting subject, but it was left to Haydn to work out this theme in the oratorio *The Creation*, of which the German text was prepared by Gottfried van Swieten. This work, one

of the greatest of its kind, was given its first performance in
the Schwarzenburg Palace, Vienna, on April 30, 1798.
The introductory "Representation of Chaos" for orchestra
alone, is among the turning points in musical history and
style. Because of its harmonic strangeness and its com-
pelling orchestration, far removed from the neat precision
of "classical" music, it heralded a new age in music: the age
of Beethoven, in which great composers began to explore
the unknown regions of human feeling and thought.
Because the music is now familiar it is difficult to realise
how, for a long time, it was regarded as "modern" music.
After a performance in Worcester, England, in 1843, a
critic of *The Musical World* (April 22, 1843) wrote as
follows:

> The Chaos is a movement of the most intricate and
> difficult character, requiring the closest attention on the
> part of every performer engaged in the execution of it,
> as the slightest slip would almost inevitably throw the
> whole into confusion, and render chaos ten times more
> chaotic.

The Creation rapidly became one of the foundation works
of the choral societies that were developing in Europe and
America at the time of its composition. (Among these one
of the most important was the Handel and Haydn Society,
of Boston, Mass., founded in 1815.)

In 1801 Haydn produced a secular oratorio, based on a
famous poem by James Thomson. This was *The Seasons*,
in which, in music that heralds the new spring of the
Romantic movement, Haydn paints charming pictures of
the country life with which he was so familiar.

In 1800 Anna Maria Haydn died. In 1805 Johann
Evangelist Haydn died. A year later Michael Haydn died,

Michael Haydn

and was buried in the Catacombs in the rocks above St Peter's Church in Salzburg (where his monument is to be seen). Michael had known distress in his last years, for in 1800 he had been robbed by the French soldiers who invaded Salzburg. But he had also enjoyed a measure of appreciation that put his somewhat nearer to his brother Josef's reputation. Nicholas of Esterház had indicated that he should succeed his brother as Director of Music at Eisenstadt. A year before his death Michael was elected to membership of the Academy of Music in Stockholm, of which Josef had become a member in 1798.

Attended by his servant and copyist, Johann Ellsler (whose daughter became one of the great European ballerinas), Josef Haydn began to put his affairs in order. He produced a catalogue of his works, and made his will (in

The performance of The Creation *in Vienna on March* 27, 1808

which many bequests show how greatly he loved his
relations and friends). His health began progressively to
deteriorate, and sometimes he fell into moods of depression.
But many visitors came to see him, both in Eisenstadt and
Vienna, and more honours were bestowed on him. In 1800
he was presented with a medal by the city of Paris. In 1803
the Magistracy of Vienna similarly commemorated his
eminence. A year later he was given the Freedom of the City.

On March 27, 1808, a performance of *The Creation* took place in Vienna. Although now very feeble, Haydn was well enough to attend. As he entered the concert hall a fanfare of trumpets was sounded. This performance was a great emotional experience for all those present. As the chorus sang the words "And there was light", the audience broke into spontaneous applause. Too tired to hear the whole of the concert, Haydn was taken away at the interval. Before he left Beethoven knelt to kiss his forehead. Haydn raised his hands to thank his friends and made as to bless them.

In 1809 the French armies invaded Austria and Vienna. As the guns bombarded the capital in May, Haydn's friends knew that he was near the end of his life. The days passed. French officers visited him to pay their respects. The last music which Haydn played was that of the Emperor's Hymn. In the night of May 31 he died.

He was buried in the parish church of Gumpendorf— from which his skull was later stolen. In 1820 the body was taken back to Eisenstadt, and in 1954 the skull, which had been in the keeping of the Music Society of Vienna, was also taken back.

Haydn's body rests in the "Church on the Hill", in Eisenstadt, which he had known so well. It is moving to visit this small Burgenland town, where Haydn's name is reverenced because he was the most notable of a family which was well known in those parts. That was where he belonged. But, as a monument on the wall of his old home states, he belonged also to the company of the world's great men. He did so because he never lost sight of his origins.

The Church on the Hill *at Eisenstadt*

Index